LOST AND FOUND

THE TITANIC AND OTHER Lost Ships

JOHN MALA

QEB

QEB Publishing

Copyright © QEB Publishing, Inc. 2011

Published in the United States by
QEB Publishing, Inc.
3 Wrigley, Suite A
Irvine, CA 92618

www.qed-publishing.co.uk

ISBN 978 1 60992 054 8

Printed in China

Project Editor Carey Scott
Designer Stefan Morris Design
Illustrations The Art Agency
and MW Digital Graphics
Picture Researcher Maria Joannou

Front cover images: The *Titanic* departing Southampton, England in April 1912 (top), and lying on the floor of the North Atlantic Ocean today (bottom).

Library of Congress Cataloging-in-Publication Data
Malam, John, 1957-
Titanic and other lost ships / John Malam.
    p. cm. -- (Lost and found)
Summary: "Describes the historical circumstances that led to ships sinking and being lost, such as the Titanic and the Civil War submarine H.L. Hunley plus the archaeological discoveries that found evidence of and preserved these shipwrecks"--Provided by publisher.
ISBN 978-1-60992-054-8 (library bound)
1. Shipwrecks--Juvenile literature. 2. Underwater archaeology--Juvenile literature. 3. Salvage archaeology--Juvenile literature. 4. Treasure troves--Juvenile literature. I. Title.
G525.M2237 2012
910.4'52--dc22

                    2011012122

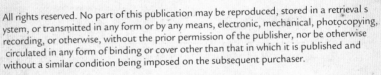

The words in **bold** are explained in the Glossary on page 31.

CONTENTS

WHAT IS A LOST SHIP?

The seabed is littered with the wrecks of tens of thousands of ships. They are the world's lost ships, and every one of them has a story to tell about a voyage that ended in disaster. However, their stories can only be told after a lost ship is found.

Ships become lost at sea for many reasons. The weather is the greatest danger of all for sea captains. Storms, giant waves, and fog are all weather hazards, and have sent many ships plunging to the seabed. Ordinary human error is also a common cause of shipwrecks. Sometimes, sailors steer their ships too close to rocks, icebergs, or other ships so that they crash into them. Piracy is a constant threat and often a real danger. And, in wartime, ships can be sunk when they come under attack from enemy fire.

▲ A marine archeologist points to an object on the seabed while surveying the site of an ancient Roman wreck off the coast of Italy.

▼ This is a reconstruction of the Uluburun ship, wrecked off the coast of Turkey 3,300 years ago. Divers spent 10 years recovering its cargo, which included elephant tusks, ostrich eggs, and hippopotamus teeth.

When a lost ship is found, the experts—**archeologists**, **salvage** operators, and professional **treasure hunter**s—can begin to recover objects from it and bring them back up into the daylight for everyone to see. In some special cases, even the ship itself is brought ashore and put on display in a museum.

▲ This 19th-century painting shows galleys—ships powered by oarsmen—in battle. Galleys were used as warships from ancient times up to the 1500s, and were frequently wrecked in sea battles.

The Kyrenia Ship

The wreck of an ancient Greek merchant vessel from the 300s BCE was discovered at the bottom of the Mediterranean Sea, off Kyrenia, Cyprus in 1965. It took archeologists two years to excavate the ship's cargo and raise what was left of her wooden hull. They worked out that the Kyrenia ship had been sailing between the Greek islands, transporting wine and almonds, in large pottery jars called amphorae, and millstones for grinding wheat and barley.

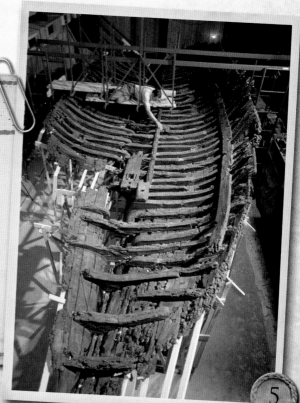

LOST:
LUXURY LINER

On April 10, 1912, the biggest and most luxurious passenger **steamship** ever built set sail from Southampton, England. The ship's name was the *Titanic*, and her destination was New York. But the liner was a doomed ship—this was to be her first and only voyage.

Location: North Atlantic Ocean
Date: April 14, 1912

▼ These second-class passengers, photographed boarding the *Titanic*, expected to enjoy a standard of luxury that only a first-class ticket would buy on other ocean liners.

On board the ocean **liner** the *Titanic* was a crew of 899, and 1,324 passengers. Among the first-class passengers were many well known wealthy businessmen. They were on their way home to the United States after visiting Europe. However, most passengers were poor people traveling third class—the cheapest tickets. They were **emigrants** who had dreams of starting new lives in the USA.

It was not to be. On Sunday, April 14, the *Titanic* received messages from nearby ships warning of icebergs in her path. The *Titanic* sailed on. Then, as midnight approached, a lookout shouted: "Iceberg, right ahead!" The collision could not be avoided, and the liner's starboard (right) side scraped against the ice mountain, splitting open her **hull** below the waterline.

► Luggage trunks and passengers boarding the *Titanic* from a ferry boat at Queenstown, Ireland. This was the liner's last stop before she sailed out into the Atlantic Ocean.

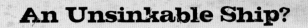

An Unsinkable Ship?

As the *Titanic* was being built, she was described as "virtually unsinkable" by her shipbuilders, Harland and Wolff. However, by the time the ship was finished, a rumor had spread that the *Titanic* really was unsinkable. But gaps had been left at the top of the liner's **bulkheads**, so the ship was not completely watertight. When water entered the hull it poured through the gaps, and the *Titanic* was doomed.

Nothing could keep the cold water from pouring through the tear in the hull, nothing could keep the ship from flooding, nothing could save the *Titanic* from sinking to the bottom of the North Atlantic Ocean. Of the 2,223 people who sailed on the *Titanic*, 1,517 drowned or died of cold in the icy water. For the 706 survivors, the night of April 14, 1912 was one they would never forget.

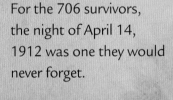

▼ As the *Titanic* sank, survivors in the water saw her stern and propellers rise up out of the water before she plunged down to the seabed.

FOUND:
THE TITANIC

The *Titanic* had sunk about 500 miles (800 kilometers) off the coast of Newfoundland, Canada, and around 2.4 miles (3.8 kilometers) down. The wreck was so deep, and so far from land, that plans to salvage the ship were not realized for a very long time.

Almost 70 years went by before a serious search to find the *Titanic* finally began. In the 1980s, US explorer Jack Grimm had three attempts at finding the wreck but failed. Someone else who dreamed of finding the *Titanic* was Robert Ballard, a US marine geologist (scientist of the seabed). He had spent years exploring the world's oceans with underwater vehicles, and in 1985 he began to examine the North Atlantic seabed, looking for the long-lost liner.

▶ The *Titanic*'s pursers looked after passengers' valuables, storing them inside leather bags such as this one. Inside were someone's keys, gold watch, and purse.

From the control room of his ship the *Knorr*, Ballard operated a tiny **submersible** vehicle named *Argo*. Far below the surface, *Argo* traveled around the seabed, filming its surroundings and sending the images back up to the *Knorr's* screens. For five weeks, Ballard stared at the screens. *Argo* found nothing. Then it filmed a large metal object on the muddy seabed. Ballard studied the pictures, and realized he was looking at a ship's boiler. *Argo* filmed all around the boiler, looking for the ship it had come from—and that's when Ballard saw the unmistakable shape of a ship on his screen. As more came into view, Ballard could see it was the *Titanic*, lost for 73 years but now found.

The Argo

The *Titanic* was found by the *Argo*, a **remotely operated vehicle**, or ROV. It was a long sled, lowered into the water by a crane from the surface ship the *Knorr*. As the *Knorr* moved along, it towed the *Argo* behind it, far below near the bottom of the ocean. On board the *Argo* were video cameras that sent moving pictures up to the *Knorr*, and powerful headlights that lit up the underwater blackness.

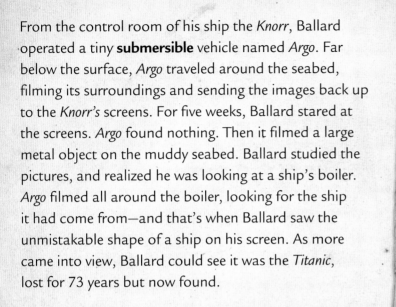

▼ Part of the deck of the *Titanic*, photographed in 2003, showing the liner's anchor chains.

LOST:
TREASURE SHIP

In September 1622, 28 ships set sail from Havana, Cuba. They were heading home to Spain, loaded with gold, silver, and precious stones. This was a Spanish **treasure fleet**, laden with valuables taken from the peoples of Central and South America.

Location: Florida Keys, USA
Date: September 5, 1622

Throughout the summer of 1622, the fleet had sailed around the Caribbean Sea, picking up its cargo of treasure. Among the fleet was a two-year-old wooden **galleon**, the *Nuestra Señora de Atocha*. The *Atocha* went to Cartagena, in present-day Colombia, and Portobello, in present-day Panama. At each port she collected a haul of treasure, filling her hold with silver, gold, and emeralds brought from across South America. By August, her hold was packed with riches, and she was ready to join the fleet on the long voyage back to Spain.

As the ships left Havana that September, all eyes were on the sky. Every sailor knew that the hurricane season was about to begin, and the last thing they wanted was to be caught in a howling storm.

▼ Two sailors lower a barrel of treasure into the hold of the *Atocha*, while a third man prepares the next load.

But that was exactly what happened. Gale-force winds battered the ships and huge waves washed over their decks. The *Atocha* was blown northward, and onto a reef. Water poured through her shattered hull. The great ship sank to the bottom, taking 260 people with her, along with 161 gold bars, 901 silver bars, 250,000 silver coins, and a large quantity of **emeralds**. When the storm was over, all that could be seen of the *Atocha* was the stump of her mast poking up above the water's surface. Clinging to it with all their strength were five men, the only survivors.

▲ An artist has captured the sinking of a Spanish treasure fleet in 1715, when all the fleet's 11 ships were wrecked in a hurricane near present-day Florida.

Treasure Ships

Spain's merchant ships were large, slow-moving vessels, which were easy prey for pirates and raiders from England, France, and the Netherlands. For safety the merchant ships always traveled together in large fleets, and were escorted by warships known as galleons. Although she carried treasure too, the *Atocha* was an escort galleon, and she was armed with 20 cannons. It was her job to protect the other ships of the treasure fleet from pirates.

FOUND:
THE ATOCHA

The treasure ship the *Atocha* sank in 1622. With her mast poking up above the waves, a Spanish salvage team had no problem finding her. Soon after she was lost, divers—holding their breath—went down to the wreck.

The divers could work for only a few minutes at a time until they had to swim back to the surface for air. They could not open the ship's cargo hatches, and the gold, silver, and emeralds remained out of reach. So the salvage team brought in pearl divers, who were trained to hold their breath longer than anyone under water. But by the time they arrived, a second hurricane had ripped the ship's mast off, and now the divers could not find the wreck. After a few months of searching, the team abandoned the operation.

◀ This magnificent cross, made from gold and emeralds, was found inside a silver jewel box on the wreck of the *Atocha*. The back of the cross is decorated with religious engravings.

Pieces of Eight

The *Atocha* was loaded with 250,000 silver coins, stored inside chests and barrels. These coins were known as "pieces of eight," a nickname often used to describe old Spanish silver coins. The nickname was used because each coin, or piece, had the same value as eight less valuable coins, called reales. Pieces of eight were made in Mexico, Peru, Colombia, and Bolivia, for use in Spain.

For the next 350 years, the *Atocha* was at the mercy of the ocean. Shifting sands washed over the wreck, her timbers broke up, and her precious cargo spilled out over the ocean floor, where it was buried under a blanket of sand. Then, in the 1970s, US treasure hunter Mel Fisher began to search for the wreck. It took him years, but in 1985 he at last found ship's timbers on the seabed. They came from the hull of the *Atocha*, and among them Fisher found 130,000 silver coins, 115 gold bars, and 315 emeralds, together with bars of silver, and gold chains and coins. This was only the beginning, and over the next few years the *Atocha* gave up more of her secrets. Fisher became a millionaire, and the *Atocha* became one of the richest shipwrecks ever found.

FACT FILE

Long "money chains" were salvaged from the *Atocha*. They were made of hundreds of gold links designed to be pulled off and used as money.

▶ A diver with objects recovered from the wreck of the *Atocha*. He is holding a plate made from pewter, a soft metal made from a mixture of tin and lead.

LOST:
CARGO SHIP

For 200 years, the ships of the Dutch East India Company transported pepper, spices, tea, tropical hardwood, and other exotic goods from Asia to Europe. Many of them were attacked by pirates or wrecked by storms, taking their crews and precious cargoes to the bottom of the ocean.

Location: Off Bintan Island, South China Sea
Date: January 3, 1752

In 1748, the *Geldermalsen* sailed from the Netherlands, bound for India, Java, and China. For two years she sailed around the South China Sea, transporting goods between these countries. Then, in 1751, she sailed to Canton (present-day Guangzhou), on the south coast of China, where she was loaded with cargo to take back to Europe. Into her great hold, packed safely inside wooden crates, went hundreds of tons of tea, 147 bars of gold, silks, spices, delicately decorated containers, and almost 250,000 pieces of fragile Chinese **porcelain**—teacups, saucers, jugs, plates, dishes, bowls, and teapots.

▼ This 19th-century painting shows small boats ferrying goods to and from an East Indiaman ship, which looks much like the *Geldermalsen*.

Chinese Porcelain

In the 1700s, Chinese craftspeople produced a fine white pottery called porcelain, which they hand-painted. It was of a much higher quality than European pottery, and was considered the height of luxury by wealthy Europeans. Chinese potters produced millions of pieces of porcelain for transportation to Europe, where it was sold at high prices.

The *Geldermalsen* began the long journey home in December 1751. It was full of risks. Pirates were a menace, and storms were a constant threat. But the *Geldermalsen* fell victim to a more routine danger—human error. On January 3, 1752, the ship's captain took the wrong course and steered the ship close to a reef, off the island of Bintan, Indonesia. The ship crashed onto the rocks and, as the waves pounded her hull, she broke up and sank. Eighty of the 112 people on board drowned. Her valuable cargo went down with her, and the *Geldermalsen* entered the record books as one of the hundreds of **merchant vessels** lost at sea.

▼ In Canton harbor, Chinese workers pack porcelain into wooden crates ready to be stored inside the hold of the *Geldermalsen*.

FOUND:
THE GELDERMALSEN

The *Geldermalsen* sank in the South China Sea in 1752. As she broke up on the ocean floor, her cargo crates moved around. Over the years, they split open and rotted away, and their contents fell out. But something else happened as well.

The tons of tea that the ship was carrying soon spilled from its crates, and the tea leaves floated down onto the thousands of pieces of fragile porcelain. They formed a soft blanket all around the precious pottery. Tucked up inside this protective layer of tea, the porcelain was safe from breaking. It stayed this way until 1985, when the wreck of the *Geldermalsen* was finally found by treasure hunter Mike Hatcher.

▶ The fine, hand-painted Chinese porcelain that Hatcher recovered from the *Geldermalsen* was as good as new. The dishes, cups, and saucers were finally ready to be sold —233 years later than planned.

Mike Hatcher

An orphan, Mike Hatcher grew up in a children's home in England. When he was 14, he was sent to live in Australia. There he learned to sail and dive, and eventually he became a marine salvor (someone who recovers the cargo from shipwrecks). In 1985 he found the *Geldermalsen* and, in 1999, he located the *Tek Sing*, a Chinese junk that sank in 1822. He is shown here with a sample of the pottery he recovered from that wreck.

It was the find of a lifetime for Hatcher. He located the wreck lying in 130 feet (40 meters) of water off the island of Bintan, Indonesia. The wreck was identified as the *Geldermalsen*, and from it Hatcher raised 170,000 pieces of porcelain, 126 gold bars, the ship's bell, and personal objects that belonged to the crew and passengers. However, it was the porcelain that grabbed people's attention. In 1986 the *Geldermalsen* porcelain was taken to Amsterdam, Holland—its original destination. There it was sold by Christie's, an international auction house, to wealthy collectors all over the world.

FACT FILE

An estimated 32,500 cups and saucers and 21 gold bars are still on board the *Geldermalsen*.

LOST:
CIVIL WAR SUBMARINE

The American **Civil War**, which took place between 1861 and 1865, was a bitter and bloody conflict. As often happens in wars, new weapons and machines were invented. A submarine was first used in warfare during the War.

Location: Off Charleston, South Carolina
Date: February 17, 1864

The submarine was called *H.L. Hunley*, after its designer and captain, Horace L. Hunley. She was a true submersible, able to dive and travel underwater, then return to the surface. The *Hunley* was 39 feet (12 meters) long, and was crewed by eight brave submariners. Seven of them turned a handle that made the propeller spin around and the eighth man steered the submarine. But there were problems from the start. While the *Hunley* was being tested, she sank twice, and the submariners drowned. But after each sinking she was raised and made ready again.

▼ Artist Conrad Chapman made this painting of the *Hunley* in 1863, when the submarine was in the dockyard at Charleston, South Carolina.

▼ This artist's impression shows the *Hunley* on her mission to sink the *Housatonic*. She carries a single torpedo, mounted at the end of a long spar or rod, which was designed to stab into the wooden hull of the enemy ship.

On February 17, 1864, the *Hunley* went on her one and only mission—to sink the *USS Housatonic*. She was armed with a **torpedo**, carried at the end of a long rod at the front of the submarine. It was packed with about 100 pounds (45 kilograms) of gunpowder. The crew fixed the torpedo to the *Housatonic*'s hull, then detonated it by pulling a cord from a safe distance. The torpedo exploded, sinking the *Housatonic* as planned. It was the first time a submarine had been used to sink an enemy ship. But something went wrong, and the *Hunley* sank too, taking the crew with her. This time, the submarine was left on the ocean floor.

Ironclads

The Civil War also saw the arrival of "ironclads." These were steam-powered ships built of iron, and they were the world's first modern battleships. They signaled the end of wooden warships driven by wind and sail. This is the *Atlanta*, an ironclad that fought on both sides of the Civil War. She began life as a steamship, but was converted to an ironclad of the Confederate States Navy. She was captured by the United States Navy and then fought on their side. Her days ended in 1869, when she was lost at sea.

FOUND:
H. L. HUNLEY

The *H.L. Hunley* was lost in 1864, and for more than 100 years no one knew where the wreck of the little submarine was. Then, in 1970, Edward Lee Spence dived into the murky waters off Charleston, South Carolina, and found more than he was expecting.

Spence was on a fishing trip, and he plunged into the cold water to free a trapped line. He followed the line down. As he tugged at it, he saw it was snagged on something manmade. It was a long, smooth metal object. Spence knew about the Hunley submarine, and as he broke the surface he called out: "I've found the *Hunley*!"

▼ At a conservation center in Charleston, the *Hunley* was put inside a tank filled with very cold water which kept microorganisms from damaging her. Part of the hull was removed, allowing archeologists to work inside the submarine.

Twenty-five years later, in 1995, divers from the National Underwater and Marine Agency mounted an expedition to raise the *Hunley*. After being underwater for so long, the submarine was partially covered by a thick layer of sand. Underwater vacuum cleaners carefully sucked the sand away, and little by little the *Hunley* was uncovered. To everyone's relief she was in good condition. The big day finally came on August 8, 2000, when the lost submarine was gently raised back up to the surface after 136 years on the bottom. On board were the remains of her crew, the eight brave men who had lost their lives way back in 1864. They were buried in 2004, in Charleston. And the *Hunley*? The submarine is also in Charleston, where it will eventually go on display in a museum.

FACT FILE

The *Hunley* sank in only about 26 feet (8 meters) of water, just beyond the entrance to Charleston Harbor.

◀ This leather purse belonged to one of the crew members of the *Hunley*. It is one of many personal belongings found on board the submarine by marine archeologists.

Lucky Gold Coin

Among the submariners' possessions that the salvage team found inside the submarine was a $20 gold coin. This had belonged to the *Hunley's* commander, Lieutenant George E. Dixon. Earlier in the Civil War, he had fought in the Battle of Shiloh, and the coin had saved his life when a bullet had bounced off it. For a lucky charm, Dixon had had the coin engraved with the words "Shiloh April 6th 1862 My life Preserver G.E.D." However, it failed to save his life a second time.

LOST:

THE KING'S FLAGSHIP

One summer day in 1545, a simple mistake caused a Tudor warship to sink close to the English shore. She could have been quickly forgotten, but she was a special ship. Her name was the *Mary Rose*, and she was King Henry VIII's flagship.

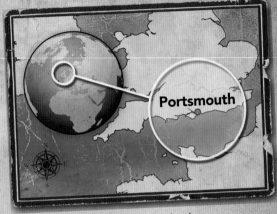

Location: Off Portsmouth, England
Date: July 19,1545

The *Mary Rose* was the pride of the English fleet. She was armed with 91 guns and had a crew of about 415 men. She had fought in sea battles against France, England's old enemy, and was about to do so again. In 1545, France sent an **armada** of 200 ships across the English Channel. They carried an invasion force of 30,000 French soldiers.

▼ The *Mary Rose* was one of the 58 ships of King Henry VIII's navy. As an official record for the king, each ship was illustrated, and its size, crew, armament, and basic equipment were described.

King Henry VIII

Henry VIII is one of England's best known monarchs. He belonged to the Tudor dynasty, a group of strong rulers who made England into a powerful nation. Henry ruled for 38 years (from 1509 to 1547). He is most famous for having six wives, and for changing England from a Catholic to a Protestant country. He was also responsible for building a powerful navy, to which the *Mary Rose* belonged.

Henry VIII ordered a defense fleet to meet the French armada. On the evening of July 19, as the French ships approached the English coast, the *Mary Rose* led the English fleet of about 80 ships out of Portsmouth harbor. Standing on the shore was King Henry VIII, who could only watch helplessly as the disaster unfolded. The *Mary Rose* had just fired its guns on one side at an enemy ship when it was caught by a strong gust of wind. As her sails filled, the *Mary Rose* leaned over, the open **gunports** dipped below the surface of the water, which quickly came rushing in. The more she leaned over the more she filled up. Nothing could be done to keep the *Mary Rose* from capsizing, and down she went, taking about 400 men to a watery grave.

▼ Horrified sailors try desperately to save themselves from drowning in the torrent of water gushing onto the deck of the *Mary Rose*.

23

FOUND:
THE MARY ROSE

FACT FILE

Only the right (starboard) side of the *Mary Rose* has survived. The left (port) side has rotted away.

The *Mary Rose* was lost just under a mile (1.5 kilometers) from Portsmouth harbor. Soon after she sank in 1545, an attempt was made to lift her, but only some cannons were raised. The warship was abandoned, and her location was forgotten.

Time passed, and the Tudor warship sank deep into the muddy ocean floor. Shipworms ate their way through her oak timbers, and powerful ocean currents pushed and pulled at her, breaking her open. Then, in 1836, fishermen complained that their nets were getting snagged on a wreck. Two local divers went to investigate. They pulled up some large guns and other items, and experts soon figured out that these came from the *Mary Rose*. But, when the divers stopped working on the wreck, its location was soon forgotten again.

▲ These gold coins are known as "angels" because they show St. Michael with angel's wings, spearing a dragon. Twenty-seven of these "angels" were found on the *Mary Rose*.

▲ Thousands of ordinary objects were found on the *Mary Rose*, revealing the everyday lives of English Tudor sailors. This set of wooden knives (right) would have had lots of uses, while the fine bone comb (left) was designed for combing out nits.

For the next 135 years, the *Mary Rose* remained at the mercy of the ocean and ships passing over her as they sailed to and from Portsmouth. Then, in 1971, an amateur diver, Alexander McKee, found the *Mary Rose* once more. A team of marine archeologists spent the next 11 years uncovering the "Tudor time capsule" McKee had found. They recovered almost 20,000 objects from the wreck, and the bones of hundreds of sailors who had drowned in the tragedy. In 1982, the *Mary Rose* herself was carefully raised. She was taken to Portsmouth, the port she had left 437 years earlier, where she went on display in a museum built specially for her.

▼ The hull of the *Mary Rose*, held inside a metal cradle, was raised from the ocean floor by a giant crane. As the cradle was lifted clear of the water, part of it collapsed onto the *Mary Rose*—but luckily the ship was not damaged.

Preserving the Mary Rose

After so long under water, the timbers of the *Mary Rose* were waterlogged. If they dried out, they would shrink and crack. For 12 years, from 1982 to 1994, she was sprayed with chilled water. This kept her damp. For the following 10 years, from 1994 to 2004, she was sprayed with a waxy chemical called polyethylene glycol (PEG). It soaked into the wood, squeezing the water out and replacing it with wax. This is how the *Mary Rose* has been preserved.

LOST:

WORLD WAR II WARSHIP

On April 28, 1942, 13 merchant vessels sailed from Murmansk, Russia. They were heading to Britain, and their journey was full of danger. It was World War II (1939–45), and ships that followed this route were likely to be attacked by German submarines.

Location: Barents Sea
Date: April 30, 1942

Merchant vessels that crossed dangerous areas sailed in fleets known as **convoys**. They were protected by escort ships, warships whose job was to fight off attackers and escort the fleet safely home. HMS *Edinburgh* was an escort ship that sailed with the convoy from Murmansk. She was a new ship, launched only four years earlier, and was heavily armed with guns and torpedoes. She was built for battle, but on this voyage the *Edinburgh* also carried a valuable cargo.

Shortly before the *Edinburgh* left Murmansk, 93 wooden boxes were loaded into her bomb room, the safest and strongest room on the ship. The boxes contained 465 bars of Russian gold, weighing five tons and valued at about $5.75 million. The gold was a payment by the Russian leader Joseph Stalin for supplies from Britain.

▼ British sailors load crates packed with gold bars inside the bomb room of HMS *Edinburgh*. The bomb room also contained crates of ammunition.

German U-Boat

German submarines are known as U-boats, from the German word *unterseeboot* which means "submarine." Germany had more than 1,100 U-boats during World War II. The U-456, the U-boat that attacked HMS *Edinburgh*, was launched in June 1941. She went on 11 patrols, sank six ships, and damaged two others. She was sunk in 1943 in the North Atlantic, after being hit by a torpedo dropped from a British plane. Her crew of 49 was all lost.

Two days into the homeward voyage, a pair of torpedoes from a German submarine slammed into the side of the warship. The badly damaged *Edinburgh* tried to return to Murmansk but she was attacked again. In the gunfire, around 60 of the crew were killed. The rest abandoned ship, and the *Edinburgh* slipped below the waves, sinking 800 feet (245 meters) to the bottom of the icy Barents Sea. She took the Russian gold with her, and because it sank at such a great depth, no one ever expected to see it again.

▲ HMS *Edinburgh* was a British light cruiser warship, armed with twelve six-inch guns and six torpedoes. She had a crew of 750. Before her final voyage, she carried out escort duties, laid mines, and took part in the search for the German battleship the *Scharnhorst*.

FOUND:
HMS EDINBURGH

HMS *Edinburgh* sank to the bottom of the Barents Sea in 1942, and her story could have ended there. But her cargo of Russian gold made her different from other World War II wrecks—it was just too valuable to be left on the ocean floor.

As the years passed, the steel hull of the British warship was attacked by rust. But gold does not tarnish, and the gold bars stored inside her bomb room stayed as shiny as the day they were made. The only change to the gold was what it was worth: it became far more valuable. By 1980 it was worth an incredible $64 million, and people were starting to wonder if it could be recovered. One of them was Keith Jessop, an Englishman who owned a company that salvaged shipwrecks.

▼ Bankers, responsible for insuring the gold, thank the organizers of the salvage expedition. In 1981, each bar was worth about $148,000.

▼ Jessop's divers used specialized cutting equipment to penerate the bomb room. Several divers were injured during the long and difficult operation.

Recovering the Gold

Because around 60 men had died on the HMS *Edinburgh*, it was designated a "war grave," which meant it should not be damaged. The British government gave Keith Jessop permission to recover the gold from HMS *Edinburgh* because he promised that his divers would not damage the wreck. Other, bigger salvage companies had asked to recover the gold, but they wanted to blast the wreck open with explosives, which would have destroyed part of the ship.

The British government gave Jessop permission to search for HMS *Edinburgh*. If he found the gold, he could keep 45 per cent as his reward. The rest would be split between the British and Russian governments. In 1981, Jessop found the *Edinburgh*. Divers cut through the armor-plated hull, and after two weeks they reached the bomb room. Of the 465 bars of Russian gold, Jessop found 431 and he became a rich man. A further 29 bars were fished up in 1986. Five bars have never been found, and they are still to this day on board the wreck of HMS *Edinburgh*.

TIMELINE
OF DISCOVERIES

1965

The *Kyrenia* ship, an ancient Greek cargo vessel from the 300s BCE, is found off the coast of Kyrenia, Cyprus.

1971

An English warship, the *Mary Rose*, lost in 1545, is found off the south coast of England. She was raised to the surface in 1982.

1981

HMS *Edinburgh*, a British warship lost in 1942 with a cargo of Russian gold bars, is found in the Barents Sea.

1982

One of the world's oldest shipwrecks is found off the coast of Uluburun in southwest Turkey.

1984

Pirate ship the *Whydah Gally* is found off Cape Cod, Massachusetts. She was lost in a storm in 1717.

1985

The wreck of the *Titanic* is located in the deep waters of the North Atlantic Ocean, where she sank in 1912.

1985

A Spanish treasure ship, the *Atocha*, lost in 1622, is found in shallow water off the Florida Keys.

1985

The *Geldermalsen*, a Dutch merchant ship loaded with Chinese porcelain, is found off the island of Bintan, Indonesia. She was lost in 1752.

1989

The *Bismarck*, a famous German battleship of World War II, is found in the Atlantic Ocean.

1995

The *H.L. Hunley*, a submarine lost in 1864 during the American Civil War, is found off the coast of Charleston, South Carolina.

1999

The *Tek Sing*, a Chinese junk carrying 1,600 passengers and a cargo of porcelain, is found in the South China Sea. The *Tek Sing* was lost in 1822. She becomes known as "China's *Titanic*."

2008

HMS *Victory*, a British warship lost in 1744 off the coast of France, is found.

2010

The world's oldest bottles of champagne and beer are found on a ship wrecked off the coast of Finland 200 years before. Experts believe they are still drinkable.

GLOSSARY

archeologist
A person who digs up and studies the remains of the past.

armada
A Spanish word for a fleet of warships.

bulkhead
A dividing wall in the hull of a ship, often creating a watertight compartment.

civil war
A war between people of the same country.

convoy
A group of ships traveling together under the protection of escort ships.

emerald
A bright-green precious stone.

emigrant
A person who leaves his or her own country to start a new life in another place.

galleon
A large ship designed to carry cargo and sometimes provide protection for other ships.

gunport
A hole in the hull of a ship through which a cannon is fired.

hull
The main part of a ship.

liner
A large passenger-carrying ship that sails along fixed routes ("lines").

merchant vessel
A ship that transports cargo.

porcelain
A hard, white pottery with a glossy surface. Also known as china.

remotely operated vehicle
An underwater vehicle, or submersible, that is operated from a ship on the surface. It is usually called an ROV.

salvage
The rescue of a wrecked or damaged ship and its cargo.

steamship
A ship powered by steam.

submersible
A small craft that operates under water, usually at great depths.

torpedo
A weapon that travels underwater and explodes on impact.

treasure fleet
Ships carrying treasure that sail together.

treasure hunter
A person who searches for treasure. Some treasure hunters (looters) damage ancient sites and break the law in their search for treasure. Others work with archeologists.

U-boat (unterseeboot)
A submarine of the German navy.

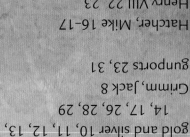

INDEX